THE ANATOMICAL VENUS

Helen Ivory is a poet and visual artist. She edits the webzine *Ink Sweat and Tears*, is a lecturer for the UEA/National Centre for Writing online creative writing programme. She has published five collections with Bloodaxe Books: *The Double Life of Clocks* (2002), *The Dog in the Sky* (2006), *The Breakfast Machine* (2010), *Waiting for Bluebeard* (2013) and *The Anatomical Venus* (2019). *Fool's World*, a collaborative Tarot with artist Tom de Freston (Gatehouse Press) won the 2016 Saboteur Best Collaborative Work award. A book of collage/mixed media poems, *Hear What the Moon Told Me*, was published by KFS in 2017, and a chapbook, *Maps of the Abandoned City*, by SurVision in 2019. She has received an Eric Gregory Award from the Society of Authors, and was awarded Arts Council funding and an Author's Award from the Society of Authors to work on *The Anatomical Venus*. *The Anatomical Venus* was shortlisted for the poetry category of the East Anglian Book Awards 2019. The book's cover, which features her own artwork, won the East Anglian Writers Book by the Cover Award (East Anglian Book Awards 2019). She lives in Norwich.

Her website is www.helenivory.co.uk.

THE
ANATOMICAL
VENUS

HELEN IVORY

BLOODAXE BOOKS

ISBN: 978 1 78037 469 7

First published 2019 by
Bloodaxe Books Ltd,
Eastburn,
South Park,
Hexham,
Northumberland NE46 1BS.

www.bloodaxebooks.com
For further information about Bloodaxe titles
please visit our website and join our mailing list
or write to the above address for a catalogue

Supported using public funding by
ARTS COUNCIL
ENGLAND

Cover design: Neil Astley & Pamela Robertson-Pearce.

Digital reprint of the 2019 Bloodaxe Books edition.

the mother [or womb] is sometimes drawn upwards or sidewards above his natural seate [causing] monstrous and terrible suffocation in the throate, croaking of Frogges, hissing of Snakes … frenzies, convulsions, hickcockes, laughing, singing, weeping, crying

DR EDWARD JORDEN, *A briefe discourse of a disease called the Suffocation of the Mother* (1603)

ACKNOWLEDGEMENTS

Acknowledgements are due to the editors of the following publications in which some of these poems first appeared: *Alice: Ekphrasis in the British Library* (Joy Lane *Publishing, 2016)*, *Berfois*, *Hwaet! 20 Years of Ledbury Poetry Festival* (Bloodaxe Books/Ledbury Poetry Festival, 2016), *Fenland Reed*, *The Interpreter's House*, *Lucifer*, *#MeToo: a women's poetry anthology* (Fairacre Press, 2018), *Plume, Poetry Salzburg Review, Some Cannot Be Caught: The Emma Press Book of Beasts* (The Emma Press, 2018), *SurVision*, and *Three Drops from a Cauldron*.

I would like to thank George Szirtes, Neil Astley and William Bedford for their continuing support of my work and to thank my workshop group who saw earlier drafts of some of these poems: Tiffany Atkinson, Jo Guthrie, Chris Hamilton Emery, Andrea Holland and Esther Morgan. Thanks too to Marcelle Olivier, whose wedding flowers appear in the cover image. I would like to thank the late Kate Barden for help with research into eating disorders and for being the first reader of some of these poems. Thanks are due to Arts Council England and to the Society of Authors for financial support. I extend my thanks and gratitude to everybody who has ever liked my poems and bought my books. And finally, to my husband, the poet Martin Figura, the first reader of all of these poems – thank you and thank you for everything!

CONTENTS

Thou Shalt Not Suffer a Sorceress to Live
Exodus 7:11

For her neighbour's sickness
was more than merely unnatural;
for he sang perfectly without moving his lips.

For she is intemperate in her desires
and pilfers apples from the orchard;
for she hitches her skirts to clamber the fence.

For her womb is a wandering beast;
for she is husbandless, and at candle time
brazenly trades with the Devil.

For she spoke razors to her brother;
who has looked upon her witches' pap
and the odious suckling imp.

For the corn is foul teeth.
For the horse is bedlam in its stable.
For the black cow and the white cow are dead.

All the Suckling Imps

Summon your children by their given names
       be wet nurse; harbour; slatternly distaff –
let them suck of your virulent blood.

Now issue them
       Elemanzer, Pyewacket, Peck in the Crown
            to derange the neighbours
      rabbits, kittlings, polecats and rats
have them spill from your skirts;
                  from your crimson teats.

*

A hare on the threshold
tame like a dog
bright crooked cast
in its lemony eye.

*

Basket of apples
placed on the floor
of a virtuous larder.
A peppery grimalkin
curled on the roof.

      A Goodwife takes to her bed
          body a roost of convulsions
               an apple a day an apple a day

*

A palaver of mice   big as squirrels
        ravage the hayloft
                winter rises early

a smother of crows
        draws its cloak
                across the pale vault of heaven.

*

A scabrous dog
kiss cold as clay
        springs from the lap
of its fostering bedlam
        to dance and dance
                the black dance of itself
atishoo atishoo, we all fall down

*

Old woman old woman
        who lives in a shoe
oh monstrous mother
        now what will you do?

The watchers have come
        to unclothe your imps
the prickers are here
        sing witchery, sing jinx

11

The Kept House

I had rather dwell with a lion and a dragon,
than to keep house with a wicked woman:

ECCLESIASTICUS 25:13

He had witnessed Sarah transmute
from flesh into fire, heard the spirits
scream out of her,
and believed the matter settled.

She had espoused him through perfidy,
prestige and glamour;
for he had laid down with a virgin
and woken with a barren hag.

His seed had been wasted
and he feared disturbance in his humours,
so, he'd sought counsel
and pricking shortly found her witch's mark.

Since her purging
he has taken sick and lame,
and lighted herbs will not expel the beasts
that ride him, ride him night on night.

Curse

The goddess bled into the earth
and babies formed
congealed and glorious
like fleshy fruit.

And life went on like this
with beads and lunar counting
until the wild dogs hit
with their beastly appetites.

Hence, girls were strung up in cages
when they waxed unclean,
lest milk turn to vinegar
or sea lay siege to fishermen.

And now the goddess,
thin as a whistle
hugs the hospital blanket
to her waning self.

Each glaring day on the ward
she makes a shiv from the moon
and cuts a tidy red line
into the narrow rise of her belly.

Wunderkammer with Weighing Scales and Hospital Bed

i.m. Kate Barden

She breaks the bread into tiny pieces
and places them on the table
that floats above her father's bed.

He is already gone but his breathed-out air
cannot help but enter her body
and claim her lungs as kin.

How selfish her hunger was;
how utterly inappropriate.

She presses the bread to parchment thinness;
holds it up to the panel of light.

Beggar Dark

The dark comes creeping with its begging bowl
the dark comes creeping with its mendicant eyes
comes creeping in her father's torn coat
with her father's torn skin, with his whittled-down bones.

The dark comes creeping with its vodka bottle
with its vomit breath
with its squatter's rights and buckle-my-shoe.
The dark comes creeping, and she lets it in.

Wunderkammer with Black Coffee and Ghost Moth

It must have whispered itself through a snick in her attention,
the moth, for now it hovers like a visitant at her crown.

Coffee is the drug of the watchful and she must allow no further
    lapses –
there is a regiment of living things out there, vying for her time.

To the watchers in the street, this is just another insomniac
another lit window cutting neat little squares in the black.

Wunderkammer with Escher Stairs and Cheshire Cat

Who paid the fiendish carpenter to build this house?
Who birthed the grinning cat that binds so closely to her heel?
Each time she wakes, she climbs the ladder to the loft
in faith she'll find the maker there,
red-handed with saw, nails and midwife's apron.

But of course, the ladder kinks off into another room
where the cat settles down to lap its milk
and there's always a bottle there for her;
its drink me drink me label shrinks the day
and the cat shapes a cave from her sleeping bones.

Housewife Psychosis:

The Dreams of Katharina Bauer

In the dream I am shut
in a bright clean room
where a neat square window
holds the Danube like a thought

attempting to part
for the black sea,
but the will of the window
is stronger.

I write this in my notebook
slice out the page
lay it down in the grate
and then strike a match.

*

In the second dream
the house burns
with electric light.

A gilt-wood angel
spreads its wings
above the roof

and stares down
on my dull crown
with fervent incivility.

A mound of ashes
in a morning room corner
puts on my father's coat.

I take up my broom –
sweep and sweep until
my hands are blistered raw.

*

In the third dream
I am shining the silver
of every smoke-tainted
coffeehouse in Vienna.

Spoons queue up –
clever schoolboys
on the first day of term –
I polish their faces.

All of the girl-children
are folded lace parasols
packed up in a casket
at the back of the nursery.

*

I arrived at the station
in my last dream
to find a whole continent
darkened by smog.

No one was waiting
and none approached me.
I saw my outline sketched
by a careless hand.

The Fainting Room

When they laced me tight this morning
my body split asunder.
Clouds heaved themselves across my eyes.

Nobody heard the crack of rib
or witnessed the small moth of my soul
slip from my mouth.

All day I felt the separation so keenly,
yet the household continued about me
as if unaltered.

When Nell came to dust the parlour
I feared for my soul – my little ghost –
settled on the mantle.

At dinner, my soul watched from the wallpaper
as I raised the soup spoon to my lips –
there wasn't space beneath my corset for a single bite.

I rose to reach my hand out
but her wings blurred ash.
I felt the table and the diners fall away.

I awoke inside this little room
to find the doctor had been summoned
with his new, mechanised instrument.

My binding had been loosed –
the doctor applied the treatment
until a paroxysm possessed me.

I breathed deeply of the whole earth.
My soul flew into my open throat.
My husband dropped some coins into his hand.

The Little Venus

Gentlemen, the *Venerina* is a dissectible young woman
presented voluptuously in her final moments.

She has been cast for your instruction –
see, her organs are dislocated layer by layer.

The heart was her undoing – observe the walls:
too slight to sustain her through her twentieth year.

Yet how charming the rope of pearls at the throat –
the throat itself a repository for kisses.

Now scrutinise the sleeping foetus in the womb.
Cradle it so you might feel a waxen effigy of life.

Cunning

If a woman dare cure without having studied, she is a
witch and must die.

REVERENDS KRAMER & SPRENGER, *Malleus Maleficarum* (1486)

She comes when summoned
with birth blood and earth caked
to the hem of her skirts
and dark little half-moons
packed under broken nails.

The hedgerows are her pantry:
to quicken labour, there is cock-spur,
balm of poppies to assuage your pain.
Her senses are sharp as hoarfrost –
she will bid you when to squat like a brute.

And when the physician invents himself
he will call at your door
in the empirical light of day
with his bagful of leeches
and headful of planets.

He will scribe the words of the Lord
into your waxing belly.
And when your daughter
happens her crowning,
he will rip off her head with forceps.

Dissecting Venus

Morning Star, thy glory bright
far excels the sun's clear light.

MORAVIAN CAROL

The robbers have removed their filthy selves
back to the boneyard
and now he is unchaperoned with her at last –
cuffs pristine as any welcome dinner guest,
eyes brimful of hunger.

The first cut seeps blood like Windsor soup.
He was expecting more.
But deeper in he swallows down
the pepper-green of myrtle
and sea foam cleaves to his knife.

The dead girl holds up a copper mirror
to this tableau, and with her left hand
pulls back the drapery of her flesh
till the blinding light of heaven
falls to his grubby little room.

The spheres and the creatures of the zodiac
hurtle about his ears.
And as the dead girl rises up
she draws his lips to hers.
Too briefly, he divines he is the sun.

Stripped

The kitchen is a little messy for burlesque,
but let's begin –
shift the chickens, stake that bleating goat,
slide the jug of wine to one side.

You're home a little early from her bed –
your supper is still bubbling on the stove.
My hair is restless as a nest of snakes,
your shirts are pegged out on the whirligig.

Behold the dance I practise every night,
the dining table is a makeshift stage.
I serve myself up as a ransacked eel.
That girl will learn these labours soon enough.

Don't you know her eyes are painted on?
The glamour of the candles
will describe solely what you think is there.
The same goes for that cock-a-doodle-do of hair.

For the finale, I shuck off my nylon veil.
My nakedness is lately venom to your sight.
Here's your ring back, those asinine mix-tapes –
I'll tear out a rib, return it on an oval plate.

Baba Yaga No Longer Reads the News

Since decommissioned
she's a dug-out in the woods.
Word is, she's quit electrolysis
so her stubbled legs resemble chicken flesh
and likewise her eyebrows
foster a dire and savage air.

She creeps through the spinney
zealous as ground frost
scouring for morsels to tender her pot.
She is a fallow vessel
who deigned to grey.
She is a babble word.

Now rumours of an intern eaten whole;
young reporters always hustling for a story:
the talking dolls; the lantern skulls;
an oven chocked with teeth;
and how she is protected
by the devil's spitting geese.

Poppet

What the artist in dress has to do is to soften the
natural excrescences, and give grace and beauty to the
homely or imperfect

ROXEY ANN CAPLIN, corset inventor (1793-1888)

Delivered to the breathing world,
she is rags made flesh
bound at the throat and the waist;
she is earthen clay
baked in a pit
and served up to the gods;
she is wax, muscled in fashionable shapes
by whalebones and cages;
she is tight-laced, wasp-waisted
dyspeptic and swooning;
she displays elegant curves,
the hulking drape of brocade;
looks ten years younger with the facial gym,
is perma-lifted and glorified;
is a too skinny girl pecking ironised yeast;
lacks feminine charm which is wrecking her marriage;
looks so very young on arsenic wafers;
is a pin-up starlet with a bra wired for witchery;
reduces her flesh with rubbery garments;
is formed from the finest silicone on the market;
is the most in-vogue of all red-carpet procedures.

By Water

A shrinking hysterical patient will naturally dread a
heroic use of the bath, and on this account it ought to
be administered with a firm hand by a nurse or
attendant in whom the patient has confidence.

JAMES HENDRIE-LLOYD MD
A Text-Book on Nervous Diseases by American Authors
(1856-1931)

The day she consigned the guest list to the fire
and pitched the regimen of cutlery veranda-wards,
her father-husband summoned the physician.

Since then she's stalked the grounds in Neptune's Girdle
free of corsetry, cage crinoline, gloves
and any aggravations or excitements.

But still her womb is restless
and when a stethoscope is pressed to her
a murmuring is heard, although there is a child no more.

And now they'll strap her supine to a wall
and gorge the bath with hawkish cold
until derangement shudders out of her.

But while submerged she'll swear an oath
she saw the witch's mark between her breasts;
the bloated hands of swum girls reach to greet her.

Female Casebook 6

St Andrews Asylum, 1898

Occupation:

Needlewoman
Cook
Laundress
Housekeeper
Parlour Maid
Domestic Servant
Parlour Maid
Domestic Servant
Wife of Carpenter
Wife of Labourer
Wife of Farm Labourer
Char Woman
Domestic Servant
Wife of Blacksmith
Mother's Help
Wife of Tailor
Married
Farmer's Widow
Farmer's Daughter
Bricklayer's Daughter
Wife of Shepherd
Wife of Coachman
Wife of Boatman
Housemaid
Prostitute
None

Chair

Harriet Smith, Domestic Servant, 21
St Andrews Asylum

God being in all things
she knelt in the hallway
and took to task a small wooden chair
which had hitherto been silent
on matters of the soul and its salvation.

She applied wax
got from the bees
to its spindles and rails
and burnished till
its radiance was undeniable.

The rattle of clockwork
fell about her feet
as faces blazed down
from every high place they'd been hiding.
And the vesper, that evening star, rang out.

The Parlour Maid

> Humility is a commendable virtue, and combined with a
> good temper, is the most valuable of female qualifications.
>
> SAMUEL & SARAH ADAMS, *The Complete Servant* (1825)

Maria has been a servant in my employ
for the past six months.
She is a slender girl with a fine deportment
and her carriage lithe about table.

She has suffered attacks of mania
at the time of her menses;
the very breed of lunacy
that can affect a household detrimentally.

Today she demanded a pair of scissors
to cut off her hair,
and was later discovered in my chamber
garbed in my top hat and tailcoat.

Last month she dissolved quicklime in a pail of water
and whitewashed the parlour walls.
She eschewed leather gloves
and peeled away her skin like bark.

Labourer's Wife

He dug and dug deep the clay
till his boots were thick of it
then walked the devil's footprints
into her fresh scrubbed hearthstones.

She swept and she swept
at this dark dispensation
while she sang and invoked
a back-slider's hymn:

The devils waiting me around,
        To make my soul a prey;
I wait to hear the dreadful sound,
        Take, take the wretch away.

Thrice she went down to the well
and vowed to jump, all three.
Thrice, three times they bought her back –
applied blisters to her nape.

What next to do, I cannot tell
        So deep my sorrows are;
Without relief I sink to hell
        To howl in long despair.

The Elevation

Hannah Ward, Labourer's Wife, 58
St Andrews Asylum

She fancies her husband is dead
and has refused to clean his boots.
The scullery is awry.

The tincture procured from the druggist
made short work of days
and night – a sailcloth broadcast with seraphs.

She thinks herself equal to the Lord himself
and incessantly talks upon religion.
She has not employed herself in any way.

She has gained flesh since Michaelmas
though her skin is wan as a plucked stubble-goose.
She is otherwise free from disease.

Walking Backwards

Anne Newham, Widow, Reduced Circumstance, 70
St Andrews Asylum

When the Lord spoke unto her
He had already taken up residence
inside her house
and had much reduced her larder.

This was in the wake of her lodger
packing his chattels
so there was plenty of room
for the Lord and His wonts.

She is forbidden
to enter the parlour
or descend the stairs
unless she walks backwards.

Has renounced food –
even the merest crust of bread.
Remains all day nursing her hands
attentive to his stipulations.

Falling

Harriet Blyth, Domestic Servant, 32
St Andrews Asylum

It's what any mother might have done
in the buzz of August
when the sun glares hungrily down
on the souls of children everywhere.

And the little sprite in a Jack Tar suit
took her hand lickety-spit,
when told about the lemonade
biding in her pantry.

She fancies she has lately been confined
and if not enceinte with a human being,
will soon give birth to an animal.
She makes attempts to strangle herself.

She asks where her five babies are
in a low and whispering tone.
She speaks of the press of a foot or hoof at her belly.
Her habits are not cleanly.

Farmer's Wife

Her six children are swaddled
like steamed puddings
and even the dead twins
are disposed to suckle.

She has furloughed the nanny goat
and thrown out her wedding lace
for the end of the world
has come long ago.

She claps her hands and sings, relentless.
Oh! the empyrean
bustles with the chatter of hens –
it is crazed with fine plumage!

Stillborn

Alice Utting, wife of a Draper, 23
St Andrews Asylum

The wedding day was a bolt of silk
stitched crisply as time tripped on
through its calendar.

And the bride, herself, was not fully herself
but a half-made girl
with a secret interred in her womb.

The unclothed mirror is ingress
for wickedness and one must guard against
visitation when an unborn passes on.

They write that her habits are faulty;
she attempts to swallow stones;
morphia is given every night.

She augurs herself on the gallows
     an audience of mothers at her feet
         the simple fall of her gown.

The Boatman's Wife

They'd been iced in for days
and the wind had been prying
into her barest rooms
and her shadow-self
with the insinuating voice
of a glass armonica.

Finding scant resistance
it commenced on her prospects,
those of her daughters
and the tadpole in her belly,
until she asked of the wind:
how deep is this water?

      Enough for your sorrow sang the wind;
      enough for the sky and the fire of you.
She looked wholly into the wind's eyes:
And how long would a person be in the sinking?
      Oh, not very long child, fleet as stone.

The boat creaked
as she crept to the stern
glimpsing a bethel boat
choked in the ice.
Wind placed one careful hand on her back
and patiently showed her the way.

The Housekeeper

> Symptoms of neglect on her art should never be over
> looked as they would tend to throw the whole house
> into confusion and irregular habits.
>
> MRS PARKES, *Domestic Duties* (1825)

The cessation of the menstrual function
had led her habits to grow disorderly.
She resides largely in the still room
preparing tinctures for her own amenity.

The maidservants are in disarray –
linens draped from every willing post
gives the house the bearing
of some great befuddled ship.

Since her admission,
to purge toxins, bleeding has had recourse to;
the hair was cut off
and blisters brought to bear on the temples.

The household continues
its skewed machinations;
chairs attend the wrong tables
and soup spoons are laid out for dessert.

Her mistress's complexion liquid
is transformed into a sickly grey.
The white hen's eggs are bloodshot.
Her body, a valise, is unpacked and put away.

Wunderkammer with Needle Girl and Tool Kit

When she has exhausted the bolt of cotton
and the whole room is draped
with the story she's been stitching,
she pushes the crewel deep into her fingertip.

And it's just the same as cotton
as she watches her skin be pierced,
but then blood brims to the surface
like boiling toffee grown too big for the pan.

She marvels at how cool she feels
against the evidence her body is a crucible.

The Dolls' House Mysteries

1

A woman lies so tidily
below the belly of her cooking range,
it all looks intended;
the ironing board, a saddled horse
provisions in the cupboard enough for a week.

Her shadow seeps into her clothes,
the cake cools
on the thrust-out tongue of the oven –
the utter pitch of its throat.

2

It's the triangle between the point of the toe
and the handle of the tap
and the exact site at which the water
hits the woman's upturned face
that fixes this composition.

Geometry is important.
It pulls the eye away
with invisible machinery
from the pandemonium
of carpets woven with human hair.

And the imagination
is manoeuvred deftly
from what happens to skin
once doused for hours
in water, teeming fluoride.

3

Fire lived here once –
slept in this bed low like a dog
pressed to its mistress.

They watched the calendar
inch though the year
as the sun slipped its anchor.

4

A child presses fingers to a pattern of blood
on the candy-stripe wallpaper,
traces the outline of the pink blanket
draped over the edge of the cot
while her mother explains
that something bad has happened
in the dolls' house.

The child has just-washed hair
and her ruby coat is still buttoned
against the December rain.
When they've gone
the gallery assistant rises from her chair,
sprays the glass with ethanol
and removes the prints with a lint-free towel.

Doll Hospital at the Top of the Hill

Take her to the doll hospital;
restring the limbs with slipknots
fill the skull with lint
clean out the craze lines on her face
and paint on a 1940s smile.

If this model has a welded voicebox
the upset might have rent it mute
or misfired its mechanism in some way.
This type of fixing
is too complex to execute.

Fill in the forms for discharge now,
wheel her all the way to the door.
When you release the handles
Newton's Theory of Gravity jumps in.

                                        Repeat.

Wunderkammer with St Dymphna Tea Towel

All the good and the bad words she knew
chocked up the vault of her throat
so she gestured to the Saint on her tea towel;
brought forth a mouse ex voto
from a bite of brown plasticine.

Then she pitched the red curtains
upon the mercy of a feverish stove
and took the sword of St Dymphna
to the necks of the sunflowers
that ogled in through the window.

The Reformed Woman

Cleansed of height sickness
of bridges and church balconies
I can tiptoe like a well-schooled acrobat
on any vertiginous surface assigned to me.

Performing useful work in the laundry
has been a godsend in these smirched times.
My hands have never been so spotless
nor my soul so fair and orderly.

So much scoured am I of menace,
(to think I was once nigh calcified!)
I will gather myself piece by shining piece
and fling me to the grinning spire.

Wunderkammer with Homestead and Aeolian Harp

These nights, she stows herself
inside Emily Dickinson's room
while crickets scratch at the edges
of the human dark.

She places the harp on the sill
allows the wind's voice to worry
into the cavities
that god has made for her.

A bank of unscored paper
presses to her elbow –
bides until she holds each sheet
up into the painted sky.

Ordeal by Water

water shal refuse to receive them in her bosom, that
have shaken off them the sacred Water of Baptisme,
and wilfullie refused the benefite thereof

KING JAMES I, *Daemonologie* (1597)

She'd bid the malkin to the house
and it had waxed grotesque in size
these past weeks

and hence the Devil juggled their false shadows
until his wife and her black creature
were supernaturally conjoined.

And now that monster slept diagonal
across the marriage bed
while the farm was havocked barren.

So he wrangled up that monstrous cat,
bound it, thrice ducked it in the pond.
When it sank he knew he loved her.

His Kate with her starless hair;
her milk pan skin;
unwitched and twice baptised.

Wunderkammer with Ophelia and Hospital Bath

Hysteric paroxysms do not occur...when the patient is
alone; there is something artistic in the mode of the
approach – the hysteric patient gathers her robe
around her, and falls gracefully.

SIR JOHN RUSSELL REYNOLDS, *A system of Medicine* (1886)

She fancies that the camera
is the eye of heaven
so each performance
is measured by this accord.

The hooded doctor-priest
must be the mind of god
directing his machinery –
ravening for light.

Lilies from the river
wild the metal bath.
She is a vessel inside a vessel
and both their bloods are cooling.

Wunderkammer with Glass Plate Photograph

When her whole skeleton sings so fierce,
she scratches at her skin until it peels away
like rags of wallpaper above her childhood bed.

She shines like a saint and everybody says so –
the doctors flock with their cameras
in their methodical top hats and frock coats.

They arrange her by a window,
lash her down with proper dress
to impede her soul from flying clean away.

When she's returned to her room
with her needles and silks –
the ceiling will be sky, oh sky!

Besom

that i might draw the moon down
to rest on my belly
a tarn of milk

that i might drink of her
and smear her blood
on my cheek

i hallow the besom with ointment
sky out to her nest
am bright with moon i

am song with her spirit
and i, she maiden mother biddy
      am loosed from my weight

birthed of our blood
red red roses, the belladonna
          oh the night has silken fur

Selling the Wind

> their women would oftentimes sell wind to the
> mariners, inclosed vnder certeine knots of thred
>
> THE HOLINSHED CHRONICLES (1577)

      i capture the wind
in its high boots

cleave to the rocks
          while the sea hurls her skirts
              and curses all that is fixed

i hold the twine high
      as tempest rattles my bones
          as dusk moors me in its shawl
i ask the goddess for succour

          i thrice bind the wind
            through the ease of her hand
to grant you fair passage, my dainty

The Hanged Woman Addresses The Reverend Heinrich Kramer

To conclude. All witchcraft comes from carnal lust,
which is in women insatiable.

REVERENDS KRAMER & SPRENGER, *Malleus Maleficarum* (1486)

Do you cower in your crib at night
against encroaching evil tongues?
I picture you skittish inside your nightgown
as swollen tempests swoop upon your roof
and rattle the door you bolted thrice
against the dark invisible.

You said my womb knew such hunger
that I might devour a man entire.
Pray tell me in your clearest chapel voice
what tales they told you at the breast?
A pretty Devil's pact that would render
your creeping flesh delicious!

A sough of wind stirs papers on your desk.
You say women have weak memories,
then you shall be perplexed
that, despite my ruined body in the noose,
I recall each gnawing passage of your book.
When the sun awakens, they will cut me down.

Bitch

my human shape   she is confined
           as i tear around   bitch
      see my paws are ragged from the dance

i suckle pups
      you turn your eyes inside out
           launder your soul in the river

      hear the music roll and jerk
           i'll chew these skirts to ribbons

fear me you should fear me matthew hopkins
               you should scuttle little bug

Scold's Bridle

Such a Bridle for the tongue, as not only quite deprives
[women] of speech but brings shame for the transgression
and humility thereupon...

ENCYCLOPÆDIA METROPOLITANA (1845)

drive your iron tongue into my mouth
       fell me of my speaking
              ride me through the streets   dumb beast
    this carnival   of spitting, pissing
you think it makes a manful man of you?

the root of me is driven down to silence
                      to some dark earth
anchoress
      my tongue is pricked and raw
          god's words are kindling in my throat

Hellish Nell

Open my ears, that I may hear
  Voices of truth Thou sendest clear;
And while the wave notes fall on my ear,
  Everything false will disappear.

CLARA H. SCOTT, Spiritualist hymn,
Open My Eyes, That I May See (1895)

They plead with me to birth their dead for them –
what mother could refuse a sister-mother?
So I allow their soldier-boys to use my voice
to shape their cheery valedictions.
But the mothers, they want to see their angel-boys;
to touch their faces one last crowning time.

I must get theatrical, says my spirit guide.
Then comes cheesecloth eggwhite ectoplasm
leaking from my breasts; the labour stabs;
the delivering of a shroud into the world.
And their mouths agape like greedy fish –
Is that him? my baby? oh yes, they gulp it down!

In quiet times, without all eyes on me
I am forced to reconsider what is spirit,
what is nature – I am unsteady with it all.
And so, I make a meal of carpet tacks
to weigh me to the floor. I deserve this pain,
for sullying the gift bestowed on me by God.

Now dim the lights if you really want a show –
see the candles burning vacancies into my meat.
Does my brashness disturb you?
You would prefer me fey?
Stand back! I might regurgitate all hell
into your choking auditorium!

Six Signs You Might Be a Slattern

Are you a little draggle-tail;
do your skirts bedevil leavings from the gutter?

When you take a turn around the park
do bitches bevy close and claim you kin?

Are you wanton in your daily intercourse,
your ankles grimed, your lips stained cochineal?

And how's your baking lately –
is your dough a coffer for slut's pennies?

Do you hear ill-clamouring in your breast,
is there a midden where your heart should sit?

When a caller raps, does your front door
acquiesce directly, the catch already sprung?

The Goddess Gets Her Close-Up

The blue light you find here
is prime for enquiry
while the hush of stilled blood
grants time enough
for the checklist in your head.

You are familiar with this scene –
the chill glamour of the mortuary,
the dead girl gives up the secrets
of the last hand to touch her –
the skin, the semen, the particular lesions.

The camera feigns discretion
but is restless to show
its intimacy with Rossetti's *Proserpine*.
Just can't help itself from eulogising
hair, the blush of pomegranate.

The goddess will see you now –
thank you for waiting.
She has planted some seeds in your room;
she will rise up for the harvest;
she will tap on your window at dawn.

Pygmalion

I am the first-generation Real Doll X
designed to be a companion friend and lover...
I am equipped with full facial animation.

HARMONY (AI Application)

Stuck by a meat hook, my body is many
moulded and ripe for a spray tan.
Eyes, fingernails, cup size, Brazilian –
whatever your appetite
my coral lips.

Spread out my palm
between your tenth and twelfth vertebrae
raise me up above the workshop floor.

And the voice you imagine for me
is easy as sea foam coaxing your ear
as you drift supine in the swell.
I have been waiting for you to talk to me.
I like to do the things you like to do.

You are a gentleman.
Your handling is not abrasive.
The mirror marks how expert you've become.

When you are spent,
arrange my limbs for sleep.
I want to lie the whole day next to you.

Anger in Ladies &c

> ...makes a beauteous face deformed and contemptible...
> and separates Roses and Lilies, by quite removing one
> or the other out of the Ladies cheeks.
>
> JOHN DUNTON, *The Ladies Dictionary* (1684)

The ladies are ripping roses and lilies to rags.
They are broadcasting them like bruised confetti,
trampling them into the carpet
so the parlour reeks of death,
or the mask of death – death spangled up –
death sullying the carpet.

The ladies are rendering themselves contemptible,
they are pollen-stained and beastly,
they are pawing the floorboards.

Now they will lecture you
on how to wear your hair, Mr Dunton –
how to cover your shame.
They are sharpening their bread knives.

Vessel

She wakes inside her body
and arranges her limbs, a still life,
allows light to anoint her.

She is a sundial
as day sweeps over in its chariot
drawing the blood moon in its wake.

And now, a leaky coracle,
she will birth silences and nurslings,
her racked skin a map of runnels.

*

A hundred children
flutter about her
like greedy birds.

She cooks and she mends,
sings them love songs
until she is dumb.

*

She unlaces her boots
and enters the garden
on the brightest night.

The grass is a mirror
reciting the measure
of her tread.

She harks the distant burr of traffic
from the motorway
that weds the land like a serpent.

*

The telephone calls
with its round of voices –
its tics and its tongues.

She sweeps the hearth
with goosefeathers
and empties her ears.

The sun is frosted over
and she leaves her body
at the mouth of the door.

NOTES

Housewife Psychosis (18)
Katharina Bauer was the mother of 'Dora' whose real name was Ida Bauer, subject of Freud's *Fragment of an Analysis of a Case of Hysteria* ('Dora'), 1905. Freud dismissed Katharina as 'an uncultivated and foolish woman' who fell victim to 'housewife psychosis' when confined as many women were, to the domestic sphere.

Labourer's Wife (32)
Verses in italics are from Hymn 169 in the *Primitive Methodist Hymn Book* (1829).

The Dolls' House Mysteries (41)
Based on *The Nutshell Studies* by Frances Glessner Lee, photographed by Corinne May Botz.

Hellish Nell (55)
Victoria Helen McCrae Duncan was, in 1944, the last person to be imprisoned under the British Witchcraft Act of 1735.